THE BUTTERFLIES OF LIFE

A POETRY COMPILATION

NASSIA POPLI

Made with ♥ on the Notion Press Platform
www.notionpress.com

Contents

Contents

Foreword

There are times when we come across some people who have a special relationship with us, and we feel as if we know them from a previous life. I have known Nassia Popli as an English Facilitator for more than 3 years now, but I truly believe I have some past-life connection with her as well. Nassia is not just a beautiful writer but also a sensitive and empathetic person. It is her own persona and her unique manner of understanding this world that is reflected in her poetry.

The first time Nassia shared her poem with me, I was mesmerised by her words and the emotions she had penned down so innocently on paper. Her poetry resonated with my own ideas and feelings, which made me realise she has a gift that can touch other hearts. From that time till now, she has matured and become a strong and confident woman who is fearless and vibrant, just like her poetry.

Her book, *Butterflies of Life*, is about those emotions that can be so momentary and elusive that we often forget about them. But the way Nassia expresses these deeper thoughts and emotions, we are given a chance to revisit them and let them tug at our hearts. She writes from her heart, and when you read her poetry, you know you have had a beautiful rendezvous with yours.

I think I was fortunate to know Nassia and watch her grow. She has a gift that few have or maybe have lost in a fast-paced world. But she not only keeps her habit of expression alive, but she also finds joy in sharing it as well.

-Osheen Rao

Introduction

This is a deeply personal journey, a testament to the fire within me. From those very first scribbles on torn-out notebook pages, creaky at the edges, to this bound collection here, they chronicle the sum of my own love, loss, and pain. I'd like to thank all those who, throughout these years, have given me strength—as much as those who have taken it away. Both are equally important in making me what I am today. I thank those who gave me the boost, and equally, I thank those who challenged me; this is the result.

Each of these poems contains a lesson I've learned, an invitation to find your own. Poetry, after all, is such a personal art, and my words are free to become your soldiers, your survivors. If you look closely, you might just find the story of a little girl who loved life. As you turn the pages, you will find her facing pain and, finally, healing and emerging with an even greater love of life.

It is all a bit overwhelming to see these pieces, spanning years of my life, compiled into this book. I am thankful for such an opportunity. Never having shared any of my poetry before with anyone and now presenting it to whoever wants to read is a very beautiful thing, one that is very liberating.

I hope, through these pages, you can see life through my eyes and take something meaningful with you in the end.

Here's to a story that keeps unfolding.

Part 1

1. The Sound of a Ride Home

I felt the music in my veins,
The sky turning black and grey.
I smiled to myself,
Feeling the vibration of every word.
She drove at a monotonous speed
Which slowly put me to sleep.
The white wires made my ears quiver,
The speed bumps after every two beats;
I closed my eyes and felt everything all at once,
The sound of my favourite song came on.
I let the words sink in at once,
As she sang "Dancing with your ghost".

The sun and clouds played hide and seek,
The high of the song reached its very peak;
I closed my eyes to find myself,

To have drifted off to her words again.

2. Home

Attachment, a philosophy to summon
Your heat to someone;
Commitment, solemnly swearing to keep
Another's soul safe
In a place we call our heart.
If only these promises
Were kept like they were made;
If only, someone swore
to help me keep, my soul,
My precious heart, safely
In theirs;
If only I had a home.

3. Death

Do you ever just wonder what sleep is?
A temporary grave? A practice of being dead?
Do you ever just think?
If sleep and death feel the same?
Does death feel like a dream?
Is it painful?
Because I know I think about it a lot,
And not just because it's intriguing.
But because it's where all the people
I unconditionally love like to go.
I want to know,
What it is about this permanent sleep
That takes away everyone
That help me avoid,
What we like to call death.

4. Then, Now, Never

Do you ever just sit?
Just stare into a blank future?
Do you ever reminisce about memories?
Wishing you were more present in them?
Do you ever just wish you could fall asleep,
Not thinking about what tomorrow holds?
I know I do. I only wish to be free,
From constant worry,
From constant planning of who,
I am going to be.
While the world ignores,
Who I am in the present.
Is it just me who watches?
Is it just me who observes?
Is it just me
Who wants to live in the now?

5. 14th May 2023

The urgency is not so urgent anymore,
The reminders are more than reminding now;
With sixty-five minutes on the clock,
Before I get to see my worth and whatnot,
What you reap is what you sow,
But what if the seeds I reaped were bad,
But the values I held awhile,
Will they matter at all?
Will any of it let me hold my heart close?
Will any of it let the pieces stay together?
Will the glue hold me together?
Or will the numbers make me shatter?
Fifty-seven now.
As the reality of the mystery sow
Grows out of my middle
Will I reap what I sow?

6. Glimpse

It's like a glimpse,
It's like the trees you see, or that one
pink house you see on the bus home;
It's like that one second
Of persisting memory
That arises from your vision;
It's life flying by,
It's realising you've grown up
after you have.
It's someone else saying it,
And your eyes go wide-
and your mouth turns round.
It's that, but now. It's rewinding life to avoid
The present which is slowly turning into the future;
Because at last:
It's just realising
That there is no going back,
It's just older, and older now.

7. October

The memories drive further,
As the bumps in the road
Crash me into them again,
As the laughs fade higher;
At every stoplight,
I turn to look back and smile;
Every green light,
Seems like a highway,
Way way, away and away ;
As the memories,
Drive further, and summers turn to winter;
As it all
Comes to its peak and ends;
Photographs and consciousness,
It's all I have left.
Because it's getting colder,
It's going further.
And the memories
Drive away,
Slowly, away from me,

With bumps and dirt roads.
The memories,
Are turning cold now;
The memories are turning cold,
Now.

8. Silence

Cloth to numb the sobs,
A dustbin full of swabs.
The blanket to warm,
Is now wet from hurt;
Silence, silence,
While the snores go on
On the other side,
Closed eyes swollen shut.
Alone again,
Alone and in pain.
The silent cries,
As my strength fails;
The bells rings,
Face red, but tears wiped.
As I play pretend,
As I play pretend again.

9. Little Belittle Me

Today, someone asked me,
"Why do you think so little of yourself?"
But little did they know,
I've spent my life being belittled by those;
Who say they love me,
Those who point out every insecurity,
When they have nothing else to say,
Those who make me miss out,
On adventures everyone else takes.
Those who make me feel guilty,
For even trying my hardest.
Little do you know,
That I spend every night,
Crying myself to sleep,
As they belittle me.

10. Quiet

Words like thorns on a rose,
Actions like those that hurt.
Left alone, 4 again,
Bathroom floor, tears wailing.
Another girl, another girl,
Another last place, another hurt.
The mistake is mine,
Because it was I who trusted;
The mistake is mine,
Now I'm left rusted;
A nail of a door,
Of a door that closes nothing,
Just like I'm empty,
Just like I feel nothing today.
Another tear, another red,
Because it once again goes unsaid.
Of course, for I remain quiet,
Because I remain quiet again.

11. Little Big Equals

Little.
What is little?
What is big?
In this stimulation of so many,
Little big things.
What's an equal?
What's a standard?
In this world of so many,
Equally standard things.
Would my heart be,
Little, big, or too much; considered?
Or would it be equal to,
Another standard.
Another picture of a beat.
Would my beauty ever be up,
To the little but big,
Image of what it is,
In this little big world.
Because my little heart,

Has a big space for love,
But will that love,
Ever be, not little or big,
But just
Enough?

12. My Congested Room

I sit in my little congested room,
Congested from the mind, that is.
With a blue pen in hand,
And a bruised heart,
I write off my sorrows,
And of whatnot;
Though not small,
My room seems so full
Yet empty at the same;
As the walls cave and trap me in
With thoughts of just scars,
I think of crying for help,
But slowly give up,
As the walls cave and trap me in.

13. A Foreign Land

An hour past the new day,
Land foreign,
Lights bright;
The sea darker than the night sky,
As the yellow and white,
And blue and green dance;
On this Saturday night.
In this foreign land,
The lights dance bright.

14. Unfit Infinity

Some infinities are bigger than others,
But yours and mine
Seem to have fit exactly;
Some infinities are equal,
But yours and mine were just two small ones;
Yours, because of the person you are,
And mine because of the person I perceive myself to be.
I wish your infinity wasn't in my universe,
I wish that mine could have been bigger,
I wish that I had understood
How beautiful my infinity was,
I wish that our infinities never met,
Because your infinity,
Was never meant to
Fit into mine.

15. Flowers

He stands at the flower shop
With roses in his heart and hand
For her, for her because it was always her;
He stands at the flower shop,
With water off the leaf tips,
And my tears off the tip of my chin,
Because I was never her,
I never will be, I think,
Because those roses in his hand
Are not mine;
I am not his.
He is hers.
And I
Will never be her.

16. Love, But Not for Me

It's so sad,
I don't think love is made for me.
I love love.
I love watching people love,
I love watching people get love,
The same love that I never get,
The same love, that no one ever accepted;
That love?
Yeah, no, it's not made for me
And it's a tragedy.

17. If I had Just Not Fallen in Love

Million empty promises,
Thousands of painful nights,
Little by little, my heart
Died after every fight.
One by one,
You picked all my pieces,
You made my infinity yours,
But not like I did yours.
What home, what love,
Taught me all the worst.
You, if I had just not fallen in love,
If I had just not fallen in love,
I wouldn't be in pain,
And my heart would be one.

18. Trash Away

Pens and papers,
Gone to waste, gone to waste.
Importance and worth,
Gone to trash, to trash;
Happy and unbroken,
Gone forever, forever.
Await, my princesses back,
Await, I want my butterflies.
For my garbage cans
Fill with memories and sad.
But they must recycle,
Must come back,
And never leave again.

19. Swear Untrue

I ask you to swear
On my life that remains,
But your hand on my head
Slips and strains,
Because you wouldn't kill me,
With the untruth;
I duck, I see the real,
Because you're unable,
To swear on my empty life
That I'd thrown away,
That I'd end in a glimpse,
But not to your lies,
Not to your untrue swear.

20. To Be Gone, Then

I hope I am forgotten
Like that tree and that branch
With leaves of winter
But that means none;
That is what I want,
Because none is so easy,
Oblivion holds no hurt,
Oblivion now holds none,
I would love to be none
I want to be.
I hope they forget,
I hope all do, if some
It will just be easier,
To be gone then.

21. River Pain

Clear, quiet skies,
Voices of happiness but not mine ,
Stones and rocks,
Such is my heart;
And the fall and cold river,
But cold just for me and no one else.
A small breeze brings,
Tears to my eyes.
Small pain,
As I sit in the winter light;
But I see happy faces,
So, I invalidate the sadness of mine,
I see happy faces that don't acknowledge mine,
I see faces,
And hearts I used to know;
As the river flows,
And sounds of notice come back,
But they didn't know,
They didn't know.

22. Me, My Mirror and I

Hair, eyes, lips, arms, ears,
A scar, which may vanish if afar,
A spot on my shoulder,
On which I rained
On another.

Is it not a lot more?
Than whom I see,
In the gore mirror?
The lenses over my eyes,
To see better,
But all I see is the wrapper,
All I see is someone who once
Wore pink and pigtails,
Who cried if mum was not home.

Why is it,
That I cannot see,
The story?
The warrior disappears,
And the ache hides
Behind the crossing rays of light.

A lot of times, I cry,
I see a flaw,

And I hear my breath divide,
With every part of my soul,
Breaking only once again.
For a flaw is immortal,
It always brings pain.

A world of so much wonder,
A world of creations astound.
Cannot bear a red dot,
If seen on a cheek round,
Feels like blue,
Blue but it still breathes.
When hearing a world like ours
Crib over someone's body.

A heart of a kind,
A mind like a bind,
Refracting all but not those
That run and feed the world.

The mirror cries too,
For now, we try to please,
For now, our mind and hearts,
Hate what we see.
As the screams await,
And the cries display;
We wonder how to fix,
Fix what is not shattered.

We wait, and wait, and wait,
To glue pieces we did not break.
A soul we did not hate,
Before the world took our smile away.

I wait for a mirror,
When one day I see my lungs,
Where I see,
What values I hold, and my heart,
Where the mistakes I made,
And the life I live,
Reflects and teaches,
Me and the world.

The scar on my lip,
Who asked the story behind it?
Our minds constrain,
Only to who has a nine-inch waist?

Words of preference,
Limit to our eyes and hair?
My moral and affairs
Hold no importance, do they?

I wonder when,
I wonder why,
I wonder who,
Could have set a bar so high.

Standards, taking the world by a storm,
Just because a mirror never lies,
But a mirror never tells the truth,
A mirror only continues to show,
Not who you are, but how you look.

My kindness, my priorities,
Continue to be a small talk,
While my tan and my hair,
Proceed to be argued over plenty.

What my home, and my future beholds,
How my love will raise,
And not the way my hair lays.

A mirror, a mirror,
Reflect, reflect,
But my voice does not echo,
My intelligence refrains.

Await, when I smile,
Await, when I shout,
Right at the picture,
That had my life a doubt,

Await when I no more cry,
Over the scar that persists,
And over anything which lord blessed me with.

Because those who know a story,
Do not remember the cover;
For those who read,
Alas, they wonder more.

For those who tear the cover,
To reveal more than the paper,
Because I continue to look in the mirror,
Because I continue to look
In to mirror.

My scar awaits,
After every day,
Waiting to see,
If I acknowledge it today.
I look into the refraction,
Slowly forming a familiar person,
Because today I smile,
And today my fingers,
Over my scar stay.
Just long enough,
To feel it's story.
The mirror does not lie,
It had yet to be repeated,
The mirror only fails to prevail,
All my dreams and demons.

Me, my mirror and I
Look at each other,

With a big teethy smile,
Because today, I did not cry,
Because today, it was just my mirror and I.

Part 2

23. My Place to Go

Grew up with no place to go,
So I went to myself, over and over,
Grew up, told to keep low,
So I worry now, if I'm a bother;
Grew up with a voice too bold,
So now I sing.
Grew up with something to say,
So here I am hoping.

Hoping to separate my demons,
From the monsters of my present,
As every time I walk into this apartment,
My loud voice and opinions
Are shut down, torn apart,
Because all you say is always right,
But I'm never not.

For why, why can you not let me,
Let me say what I want,
Once a year not much,
Here you are to shut me down,haunt.

I wait to leave,
As soon as I reach,
I regret every word I say,
Because you make me,
But I will write and sing,
And scream and shout,
Till my suppressed perspective,
Is not suppressed about,
Because even though,
I grew up with no voice to show,
I am not your shadow.

24. Blue

I once read, heard maybe,
And it made me ponder:
How can one be so blue?
How is a colour so deep?
A colour of the evergoing sky,
One of the undergoing sea,
But still inhaling,
Still expanding,
Lungs like trees,
Still meandering,
How can blue
Still breathe?
How am I so blue
But still breathing?

25. Many Days Go By

In this world of people,
So less, but so more;
In this world of pain,
So more, so more,
With frowns and tears,
Smothering faces with fears;
I wish fear meant ghosts,
But now it means so much more.
Fear means abandonment now,
Fear means lost;
It means not a drop of trust,
It means fear of hurt.
I miss the times fear,
Meant of the dark.
Because fear now,
Is just the feel of dark.

26. My Faded Window

As the faded window glass
Appears me to a world of harass.
Harass of feelings, ever so delicate
Of times and shadows of only hate.

The window hurts,
Because of drops of rain
That make it cry,
And the branches,
Feel the hollow soul,
Of nothing but the dark sky.

Not mine know else,
Not mine knows hence;
Hurt keeps on hurting,
Like years of seasons.

Like my August of pain,
And the next of more.
I look outside my faded window,
And feel all it's sorrows.

27. An Untold Story

The cut on my lip,
The story behind a scar,
The pain behind my eyes,
The broken heart with my smile.
A story untold,
My favourite to tell,
But to who?
Who cared enough to ask,
Why my eyes turn horror,
Or my bitten tongue bleeds?
When you speak of that one,
Torturous debate.
Why, how and when is only,
Just so little,
If only my little things mattered,
But to who?

28. I Hope You Understand

Please understand,
I hope you understand,
Try to understand;
Every time it was I,
It was always,
Me understanding.

It was always,
"Hey I'm gonna go for a while,"
It was always,
"Please try to understand."
But when, I understood,
When I let you go,
I would have never,
Imagined that, letting you go,
Could mean forever.
Because when
You texted me,
That one last time,
And forgive me for saying this,
But I don't understand this time.
I didn't. I will never,
For the "please understand",
Was impossible to.
And now I've lost you,

And I'm sorry,
But I don't understand,
I just don't understand.

29. I Think of You Often

I think of you often,
Of the smile that faded too quick,
And that hug that lasted not long.
I think of you often,
The times you held my hand,
And the days I called you to cry.
I think of you often,
Because our love had begun,
But you ran to fly.
I think of you,
In the flowers, the trees,
But they wilt further tonight.
I think of you,
When hurt and pain,
Subsides and resides.
I think of you,
Now when,
Nothing you did, remains alive.
I think of you,
To hold on to something,
That sits up high.
I think of you,
As you shine as a star,
In this dark blue sky.
Funeral to our love,

But had it not been yours,
It would still happen,
As I think of you often,
Fairly too often,
And I smile and cry.

30. Rain

When it rains,
It seems to rain just for me.
Every drop seems like a tear
From the sky, sent for me.
Because when the sky cries,
I assume it's you saying hi;
Long time since you rained,
I missed you,
I'm so happy to see you today,
I hope it never stops raining,
And we can wave at each other forever.

31. Lost in the Rain

Drops snarked each window,
Pain my heart.
Each glimpse of you,
Of what I lost,
Of what I thought I had.
Little tip toes,
Of what sounded like-
Bells, but of your faded laughs.
Old faded photos,
And I lost the person,
Or perhaps I forgot,
As the drops of rain
Bring back all the pain,
I realize that I forgot thee,
I forgot all glee.
Because for me,
Without you,
There is no happy.
Without you,
There is no happy.

32. Empty

As the emptiness creeps its way back into my heart,
I wonder if I'll ever be okay,
While my thoughts go back to their darkness
And my smile fades to it's lightest
I find myself thinking;
Curious, really, to understand what it is about people that I just cannot seem to figure out
Just because I fall far from the crowd
Does it mean I deserve this injustice?
How far will I fall if I let my thoughts about
Without the hiding, without the mask
I will never understand the sense of social dilemma This world finds the need to maintain.
Am I the wrong one out of the crowd,
Or is it the world that needs to change?

33. Crumbled Papers

Crumbled papers,
Pressed with “I’m sorry”.
As every, “I’m sorry” tears,
Pieces and shatters a body.
One heart it was to cut for,
Taken away by a favourite soul.
But what is favourite?
When the hurt it causes is not known.
When unaware seems just a word,
And a song is sung but not heard.
When happy is cut away from you,
Like that paper heart you made for him.
But did you ask before taking my paper?
Taking my scissors,
To cut away my soul.
Because all you said was sorry;
Knowing a crumbled paper
Will forever be crumbled.
For you fix
My crumbles, with apologies,
But I only crumble away to sleep.

34. Dolor

Flowers so blue,
But blue of the dark, scary sea,
Voices so subtle,
But any startle me.
A pumping heart,
Pumps no more.
A throbbing chest,
Just hurts, so sore,
Deserve, do I, oh I,
Do I deserve this hurt?
The world stops,
Feels so unreal.
Numbness, over and over,
I think I deserve all this hurt.
A word and the hurt came,
A word from her came.
Stomach so full,
Of the heart that dropped so low.
No tears,
As her words just echo.

Oh, oh, will I feel like this forever?
Oh, my arms bleed, my heart shattered,
I deserve to feel so,
Don't I deserve this?

As the walls come down,
All down onto me.
And the flowers bloom black,
And the mirror so hazy,
I deserve all the pain,
All the pain she causes me.

35. The Poplar Tree

With carves and promises empty,
And a wait for her, a wait so lonely,
But promises broken, break time and over,
She passes her time with no signs of sober.
Tall and slender, not her heart, but plant,
Sleek and broken, not her hopes and plans.

Merely weak, the strings broken of heart,
Simply incomplete lives Mariana in her tower,
For I should be called Mariana,
But I wait for no lover.
I hold no tower, no power, no dowry,
For I exist simply along promises and Poplar trees.

Amongst a people-full world,
The broken me awaits for home.
As the leaves of my Poplar tree swirl,
I find not being able to rhyme with home.
Since home, a word and place unusual,
Filled with twigs and leaves, many hearts broken.
Under the shade and ice of my Poplar,
Noises silent, as if wanting my pulse,
I long and long, longer than her,
The present to past, the past turns tense,
Fields forlorn, crops no more sore.

Await, await, aweary, aweary,
No, wait, a home, just a tree
Stands tall but broken from past,
Like me, my demise, a shadow cast.
A tree of words, blood-ridden I see,
Out my window waits no lover, but just a Poplar tree.

36. Rejection

What feels a sting ?
What feels incomplete?
A ring with no caller,
A vibration without a text.
But is it the pit in my stomach,
And the pain in my head?
I think it's called rejection instead,
When never before,
But now turns ever.
Ever so hurtful,
That the blood keeps flowing.
I think it's called Rejection.

37. Happy Might have Been a Dream

Many days go by,
Many hours,
Loads of minutes,
Months, years even ;

Nothing at one velocity,
Not even the stars,
Not even that one people tree,
That stood in the middle of the city.
The kids grew up,
The time continues to fly.
My neighbours died,
And slowly, so did I.

A soul of hurt,
Of pain, and lust for dirt,
Love for ache,
Living for its sake;
From cartoons and cricket,
To wanting a one-way ticket;
From heaven to hell,
From past to now.
I stand here,
With knees broken,

And a heart fractured deep.

As many days go by,
I wonder if I'll ever find my happy.
The princesses grew up, too,
But so did we.
It's only now it hurts,
To realise,
Happy might have been a dream.

38. Faded Butterfly

From chasing butterflies
In that park that harboured our childhood ,
To five years since it went seen,
By my pair of eyes that grew.
But how can eyes grow?
They remain as big my darling,
But just grew sadder;
They remain as brown as ever,
But just tearier than dry;
As they blinked, and here,
A glimpse of faded butterflies.
Now I realise, when maa said,
"You grew up so fast,"
Here I am, still searching,
For meaning not for butterflies;
But life is flying,
Faster than those I chased.
Here am I,
Running after dreams.
Which as I blinked;
Went from yellow to gray.
All the firsts have fluttered,
Now the lasts come forth.
A day faster than last
To keep it I stutter.

All endings are beginnings,
But why has this beginning,
Begun to hurt?
My big, teary brown eyes,
Search the hallways,
For one last butterfly,
Before we part ways.

39. Pain Means Nothing

I don't flinch anymore,
Like pain, means nothing.
Nothing means pain,
To my body, to my scars.
Have so many,
Dealt so much.
That even pain,
Of a broken bone,
Or yet a broken heart,
Means nothing.
Tolerance, some call it,
I call it nothing.
Strong, some call it,
I call it pain.
Because, strong,
Means nothing,
But so does pain.

40. A Mistake

You know how mistakes are made?
Like that feeling of guilt.
And that moment of despair,
But not to yourself, not aware.
You feel the pain is caused,
By only the world,
Not you, not yourself,
But it is you,
Your heart makes a mistake.
And yet you fail,
To take it back,
To make it right.
And just like that,
A mistake is your entire life.

41. Happiness that I Hardly ever Get

And once again, I sit at home,
As you hold my neck,
And deprive me of any happiness,
That I hardly ever get.
Of the pain that I always suffer,
You force it into my heart.
And my hate for you grows,
Because what's a guardian like you.
You don't know to love,
But only provide me with pain.
You take and only suffocate,
And I give and bare.
I give and suffer and hurt,
And you deprive me.
I am so tired, of being the one,
The only one that lives like 8 at 16;
The hurt grows every day,
Because you deprive me.
And then you wonder why,
My thighs are burnt and cut,
And why I need pills to not hand myself.

You wonder what you do wrong,
So here it is ,

This, this is what you do wrong:
You're so busy not letting me go,
And so busy not letting me go wrong,
For mistakes, turn to experiences,
But no matter how hard I try,
You seem to put hands on your ears,
Or a chip in your brain,
All that can't let me live ,
All that doesn't want to make me ,
Because you, deprive me,
Of any happiness,
That I hardly ever get.

42. Muffled Pain

The dew so dense,
The pain is too.
My fogged-up lens,
As I long for you.
My tired empty heart
Demands a break,
As it breaks again,
As it pains today;
I muffle my sobs,
Under the hood of cold,
As I long for home,
Long for, A home.

43. A Train Ride

Feet set out,
Finding platforms,
Tracks white and grey,
As people walk their subways,
Set out to have a journey,
Set out to say goodbyes.
Reds and whites,
Splattered like paint.
Sun rise, rises slowly,
Rays disperse like array.
I find myself going on a journey.
But still feeling like,
I have nowhere to go really.

44. A Trip to End

Like a film
Of memories and pictures ,
We hold ourselves together;
Like pieces of this puzzle
That comes to an end,
And a part of us,
Ends with it, too;
As we head back to life,
Leaving behind,
Our wrongs and rights.
With doubts in our minds,
Of when we will get this chance
Ever again in life;
We go home feeling empty,
But with so many stories.
In our cameras
That document our own movies.

www.ingramcontent.com/pod-product-compliance
Lightning Source LLC
Chambersburg PA
CBHW031648170726
47990CB00019B/2884
* 9 7 9 8 8 9 5 5 6 8 8 0 4 *